All Scripture references taken from the KJV of the Holy Bible, unless otherwise indicated.

THE HOLIDAY WARFARE EDITION: *Surviving Family Gatherings All Year Long*: A PRAYER MANUAL

by Dr. Marlene Miles

Freshwater Press 2025

Freshwaterpress9@gmail.com

ISBN: 978-1-967860-88-3

Paperback Version

Copyright 2025, Dr. Marlene Miles. All rights reserved. No part of this book may be reproduced, distributed, or transmitted by any means or in any means including photocopying, recording or other electronic or mechanical methods without prior written permission of the publisher except in the case of brief publications or critical reviews.

DEDICATION

To our mothers—
who gave what they could,
carried what they never healed,
and loved with the tools they had.
And to every child now walking in healing and truth—
may God restore what was broken
and bless what is yet to be built.

Table of Contents

Introduction 14

FROM THE AUTHOR .. Error! Bookmark not defined.

HOLIDAY WARFARE PRAYER #1 .... Error! Bookmark not defined.

HOLIDAY WARFARE PRAYER #2 .... Error! Bookmark not defined.

HOLIDAY WARFARE PRAYER #3 .... Error! Bookmark not defined.

HOLIDAY WARFARE PRAYER #4 .... Error! Bookmark not defined.

HOLIDAY WARFARE PRAYER #5 .... Error! Bookmark not defined.

HOLIDAY WARFARE PRAYER #6 .... Error! Bookmark not defined.

HOLIDAY WARFARE PRAYER #7 .... Error! Bookmark not defined.

HOLIDAY WARFARE PRAYER #8 .... Error! Bookmark not defined.

HOLIDAY WARFARE PRAYER #9 .... Error! Bookmark not defined.

HOLIDAY WARFARE PRAYER #10 .. Error! Bookmark not defined.

THE RED SECTION Family Interrogation Warfare Prayers .... Error! Bookmark not defined.

The "What Are You Driving Now?" Defense Prayer .... Error! Bookmark not defined.

The "You Still Work in the Same Place?" Deflector Prayer .... Error! Bookmark not defined.

The "Where Did You Get That Outfit?" Surveillance Prayer .... Error! Bookmark not defined.

The "Can I Borrow Some Money?" Protection Prayer .... Error! Bookmark not defined.

The "What Did Your Kids Get for Christmas?" Armor Prayer .... Error! Bookmark not defined.

The "Oh... Did Your Kid Get a New Bike?" Rebuttal Prayer .... Error! Bookmark not defined.

The "Oh... You Gained Weight?" Blocking Prayer .... Error! Bookmark not defined.

The "Oh Wow! You Lost Weight!" Discernment Prayer .... Error! Bookmark not defined.

The "Sizing Me Up From Head to Toe" Spiritual Repellent.................. Error! Bookmark not defined.

The "Why Is My Body Your Business?" Armor Prayer .... Error! Bookmark not defined.

The "Let Me Eat in Peace" Holiday Table Prayer .... Error! Bookmark not defined.

BONUS: Leftovers Etiquette... Error! Bookmark not defined.

The Ultimate "Sizing Me Up" Shutdown Blessing .... Error! Bookmark not defined.

BONUS: Help Me Wash These Dishes & Clean This Kitchen .... Error! Bookmark not defined.

RELATIONSHIP, HAIR, HEALTH & LIFE DECISIONS .... Error! Bookmark not defined.

The "So... You Dating Anybody Yet?" Interrogation Neutralizer .... Error! Bookmark not defined.

The "When You Having Kids?" Fertility Fortress Prayer .... Error! Bookmark not defined.

The "When Are You Having MORE Kids?" Capacity Prayer .... Error! Bookmark not defined.

The "Why You Still Single?" Self-Worth Armor .... Error! Bookmark not defined.

"Why Did You Cut Your Hair?" Identity Protection Prayer .... Error! Bookmark not defined.

The "You Look Tired..." Emotional Ambush Defense .... Error! Bookmark not defined.

The "You Doing Okay Financially?" Privacy Shield Prayer .... Error! Bookmark not defined.

The "When You Getting a House?" Expectation Eviction Prayer .... Error! Bookmark not defined.

The "Is That ALL You're Eating?" Food-Shaming Firewall .... Error! Bookmark not defined.

The "Whatever Happened With Your Ex?" Resurrection Refusal Prayer .. **Error! Bookmark not defined.**

The "What Are You Doing With Your Life Now?" Purpose Protection Prayer ..... **Error! Bookmark not defined.**

The "Oh, So You Think You're Better Than Us Now?" Warfare Reversal .... **Error! Bookmark not defined.**

"You Acting Funny" Reflection Prayer .... **Error! Bookmark not defined.**

The "When You Getting a Real Job?" Identity Anchor Prayer .... **Error! Bookmark not defined.**

The "You Changed..." Release Prayer .... **Error! Bookmark not defined.**

The "You Always So Sensitive" Emotional Validation Prayer ...... **Error! Bookmark not defined.**

The "What Happened to the Old You?" Deliverance Declaration .... **Error! Bookmark not defined.**

The "Who Do You Think You Are?" Identity Explosion Prayer .... **Error! Bookmark not defined.**

The "You Still in School?" Educational Endurance Prayer .... **Error! Bookmark not defined.**

The "When You Gonna Finish?" Patience Prayer .... **Error! Bookmark not defined.**

The "Are You Still a CPA or Whatever You Studied?" Identity Clarifier .... Error! Bookmark not defined.

The "Is That Your Real Hair?" Self-Confidence Shield .... Error! Bookmark not defined.

The "Is That Your Real Hair Color?" Personal Space Protection Prayer .... Error! Bookmark not defined.

The "Oh, Your Husband Didn't Come With You?" Independence Prayer Error! Bookmark not defined.

The "Your Kids Doing Okay in School?" Gradebook Privacy Prayer .... Error! Bookmark not defined.

The "So... Why Your Child Got That Gift?" Comparison Disarming Prayer Error! Bookmark not defined.

PRAYERS FOR WHY YOU DON'T WANT TO GO HOME FOR THE HOLIDAYS ..... Error! Bookmark not defined.

"Lord, I Don't Want to Go Because My Peace Is Too Expensive" .... Error! Bookmark not defined.

"Lord, I Don't Want to Go Because I'm Tired of Being Triggered" .... Error! Bookmark not defined.

"Lord, I Don't Want to Go Because I'm Always the One Giving, Not Receiving" .... Error! Bookmark not defined.

BONUS: "Lord, Deliver Me From Parents, Aunties, Uncles & Elders Who Still Blame Me For Stuff I Didn't Do and that I am Not Responsible for that happened in Childhood." .... Error! Bookmark not defined.

"Lord, I Don't Want to Go Because I'm Not the Same Person I Used to Be" .... Error! Bookmark not defined.

"Lord, I Don't Want to Go Because I Feel Alone When I'm There" .... Error! Bookmark not defined.

"Lord, I Don't Want to Go Because the Conversations Drain Me" .... Error! Bookmark not defined.

"Lord, I Don't Want to Go Because I'm Healing From Them" .... Error! Bookmark not defined.

"Lord, I Don't Want to Go Because They Don't Respect My Boundaries" .... Error! Bookmark not defined.

"Lord, I Don't Want to Go Because I'm Better When I Stay Away" ... Error! Bookmark not defined.

"Lord, I Don't Want to Go Because I Don't Want to Pretend Anymore" .... Error! Bookmark not defined.

IT *IS* A BEAUTY PAGEANT — but for SURVIVAL, not crowns. .... Error! Bookmark not defined.

"Lord, I'm Smiling Like It's a Beauty Pageant and I Didn't Even Sign Up". Error! Bookmark not defined.

CULINARY INTERROGATION & BACKHANDED COMMENTS .... Error! Bookmark not defined.

"Lord, They Just Asked If I Cooked This" .... Error! Bookmark not defined.

"Lord, They Staring at the Food Like It's an Alien" .... Error! Bookmark not defined.

"Lord, Why They Asking What I Put in It Like It's a Crime Scene?" .... Error! Bookmark not defined.

"Lord, They Just Asked Me 'What Is Anise?'" . Error! Bookmark not defined.

"Lord, They Just Called Me Weird..." .... Error! Bookmark not defined.

BONUS PRAYER — "Lord, Protect Me From People Who Don't Season Food" .... Error! Bookmark not defined.

KITCHEN WARFARE: THE EXTENDED EDITION .... Error! Bookmark not defined.

"Lord, They Just Said 'Who Made the Potato Salad?'" .... Error! Bookmark not defined.

"Lord, They Just Said, 'Why Does Your Food Look Like That?' .... Error! Bookmark not defined.

"Lord, They Said 'This Tastes... Interesting.'" . Error! Bookmark not defined.

"Lord, They Asked If I 'Even Know How to Cook. .... Error! Bookmark not defined.

"Lord, They Said 'My Mama Doesn't Make It Like This.'" .... Error! Bookmark not defined.

"Lord, They Put Raisins in Their Potato Salad and Now I'm Concerned" Error! Bookmark not defined.

THE GUILT TRIP PRAYER SERIES ... Error! Bookmark not defined.

"Lord, They Just Said, 'You Didn't Get Momma a Gift?'" .... Error! Bookmark not defined.

"Lord, They Want to Compare Gifts Now..." ... Error! Bookmark not defined.

"Lord, I'm Being Guilt-Tripped About Not Buying Enough" .... Error! Bookmark not defined.

"Lord, They're Making My Gift About THEM" . Error! Bookmark not defined.

"Lord, I'm Just Trying to Celebrate—Not Get Shamed" .... Error! Bookmark not defined.

"Lord, They Just Said: 'Why Didn't You Call Momma?' .... Error! Bookmark not defined.

"Lord, They Said: 'Momma Misses You.'" .... Error! Bookmark not defined.

"Lord, They Said: 'Momma Was Asking About You...'" .... Error! Bookmark not defined.

"Lord, They Said: 'Momma Worried About You'" .... Error! Bookmark not defined.

"Lord, They Asked: 'Why You Don't Come Around Anymore?'" .... Error! Bookmark not defined.

"Lord, They Said: 'Momma Thinks You Don't Care.'" .... Error! Bookmark not defined.

"Lord, They Said: 'Everybody Else Calls Momma But YOU.'" .... Error! Bookmark not defined.

"Lord, They Said: 'Momma Getting Old... You Need to Do Better.'" .... Error! Bookmark not defined.

"Lord, They Hit Me With: 'You Know You Her Favorite...'" .... Error! Bookmark not defined.

"Lord, They Said: 'Momma Cried Because You Didn't Call.'" .... Error! Bookmark not defined.

PRAYER SERIES: THE "WHO'S GONNA BE THERE?" CALL TO MOMMA .... Error! Bookmark not defined.

"Lord, Before I Commit, I Need to Know Who's Gonna Be There" ...... Error! Bookmark not defined.

"Lord, If Momma Hesitates Before Answering..." .... Error! Bookmark not defined.

"Lord, If THAT Person Is Going to Be There..." Error! Bookmark not defined.

"Lord, If Momma Says: 'Everybody Coming... Error! Bookmark not defined.

"Lord, If Momma Forgets to Mention Someone... and They Show Up Anyway" ... Error! Bookmark not defined.

"Lord, If Cousin Chaos Is Coming…" .... Error! Bookmark not defined.

"Lord, If Momma Drops a Surprise Name at the End…" .... Error! Bookmark not defined.

"Lord, If Momma Says: 'It'll Be Nice to See You…'" .... Error! Bookmark not defined.

"Prayer for the Courage to Say: 'I'll Think About It'" .... Error! Bookmark not defined.

"Bless Momma for Telling Me the Truth" .... Error! Bookmark not defined.

"Lord… Why Is My EX Coming to Thanksgiving Dinner at OUR House?" .... Error! Bookmark not defined.

BONUS PRAYER — "Lord, Whoever Invited My Ex… Touch Them." .... Error! Bookmark not defined.

My Ex Is Trying to Impress My Family .... Error! Bookmark not defined.

BONUS PRAYER — "Lord… Why Did They Introduce My Ex AND My New Partner Like It's a Group Project?" .... Error! Bookmark not defined.

My Auntie Is Too Much: Look At Her .... Error! Bookmark not defined.

"Lord… Why Does My Family Act Like My Ex Is Still Part of the Bloodline?" .... Error! Bookmark not defined.

My Ex Is Remembering Good Times That NEVER Happened .... Error! Bookmark not defined.

"My Ex Just Told a Story That DEFINITELY Didn't Happen" .... Error! Bookmark not defined.

"Lord... Why Does My Ex Think We Were Healthier Than We Were?" .... Error! Bookmark not defined.

BONUS PRAYER — "Lord... Help Me Not Correct the Lies in Front of the Family." .... Error! Bookmark not defined.

The Doorbell Just Rang. My Ex's Parents Are Here. But, Why? .... Error! Bookmark not defined.

"Lord... Why Did My Family Let My Ex's Parents IN?!" .... Error! Bookmark not defined.

"What If They Came to Win Me Back?" .... Error! Bookmark not defined.

My Ex's Parents Brought GIFTSError! Bookmark not defined.

Why Did They Say I'm STILL Part of the Family?" .... Error! Bookmark not defined.

They Are Taking PICTURES Like This Is a Reunion .... Error! Bookmark not defined.

"Lord... Why Is Somebody Crying?" .... Error! Bookmark not defined.

This Feels Like an InterventionError! Bookmark not defined.

"Lord... WHY DO THEY STILL HAVE MY PICTURE UP IN THE LIVING ROOM???" ...... Error! Bookmark not defined.

FINAL PRAYER — "Lord... Thank You for Telling Me NOT to Go That Other Time .... Error! Bookmark not defined.

CLOSING DECLARATIONS...... Error! Bookmark not defined.

DEAR READER .... Error! Bookmark not defined.

Prayer Books by this Author 132

About the Author 138

THE HOLIDAY WARFARE EDITION

Surviving Family Gatherings All Year Long: A PRAYER MANUAL

Introduction

LISTEN… you gotta start in September to be prayed up for the family holidays.

Family holidays may bring out the best memories, but not always the best manners. They can bring out old wounds, old rivalries and even the cousin who's "saved until she opens her mouth." It brings out the uncle who thinks he's a prophet as soon as he starts drinking brown liquor, the sister who competes with your eyelashes and the other cousins who walk in with attitudes like its fashion. And then there's the auntie who throws shade so smooth you don't realize it hit you until next Tuesday.

The *"How you been?"* with an undertone of *"I hope you fell off,"* the loud one, the quiet one, the one who suddenly remembers they don't like you, the one who pretends they do. And then the complainers, "The food ain't even hot yet." Don't NOBODY need that kind of spiritual warfare on an empty stomach.

So YES — you start in SEPTEMBER.
By Thanksgiving, you're armored like Ephesians 6.
By Christmas, you're floating in the Spirit.
By New Year's, you've ascended.

Honestly? Y'all need the Holiday Warfare Edition. It's not just for Christmas or Easter. It's not even just for holidays, you can use it to prepare for the summer cookout, because you know who's going to be there: Everybody.

Because people think they're alone in this. Oh, no, you are not. Some think that they're "too sensitive." They think they "should be over it." But how are you going to be over something if they bring up that something every time the family gets together?

NO. Family wounds are real.
And family gatherings re-open them like they're on autopilot.

Introducing… THE HOLIDAY WARFARE EDITION

Prayers for Surviving Family Functions, Restoring Your Peace, Maintaining Sanity, and Not Catching a Charge.

There are some serious parts to this book and some funny parts too. These contents are delivered with humor but ALSO fully anointed and spiritually potent.

FROM THE AUTHOR

Family is beautiful…
Family is complicated…
Family is hilarious…
And sometimes, family requires *full spiritual armor*.

I wrote this manual because I've lived through the questions, the comments, the comparisons, the shade, the holiday chaos, and the unexpected emotional hits that seem to come out of nowhere—especially when you haven't seen folks in a while.

I know what it feels like to love your family deeply… and still need to **pray hard** before walking in the door.

This manual blends humor with honesty, because sometimes we laugh to keep from crying. But it also blends prayer with power, because God heals the wounds we never talk about. He heals family wounds, holiday wounds, comparison wounds, childhood wounds, and the wounds reopened by people who ask questions they have no business asking.

My hope is that this book helps you:

- maintain your peace
- protect your boundaries
- release pressure
- stay spiritually grounded
- respond with grace
- and walk away whole

Whether your family is joyful, dramatic, unpredictable, or a mix of all three… these prayers are for you.

And if you start using them in September?
Just know…
I understand.

Be blessed, be covered, and may your holidays (and every gathering) be drama-free, peaceful, and filled with the strength of God.

— *Dr. Marlene Miles*

Here we go!

HOLIDAY WARFARE PRAYER #1

Lord, as the holidays approach, clothe me in the full armor of God.
Not the Dollar Tree armor — the REAL armor.

Guard my heart from old wounds.
Guard my mind from their comments.
Guard my peace from family chaos.
Guard my spirit from ancestral foolishness.

Lord, help me not to engage in emotional battles disguised as:

- "Well you've gained weight."
- "So when you gonna get married?"
- "Your cousin just bought a house, what you doing?"**

Lord, put holy duct tape over my mouth if necessary.
Give me grace, wisdom, and a side dish of peace.
Let me sit at the table like a calm child of God,
not a triggered version of my younger self.

Bless this house, this food, these people…
and my self-control.
In Jesus' Name. Amen.

HOLIDAY WARFARE PRAYER #2

The Christmas Gathering Protection Prayer

Lord, for this Christmas gathering, assign angels to every doorway.
Let peace sit in every chair.
Let arguments stay in the car.
Let comparison stay at home.

Lord, cover me from old family patterns, old emotional roles, old dynamics, old spiritual attacks.

Keep me invisible to drama,
immune to foolishness,
and insulated from dysfunction.

Let me enjoy what's good—
the joy, the laughter, the food—
and release what is toxic.

Let the Holy Ghost hover over this house
like He hovered over the waters in Genesis 1.
Bring order to chaos.

Bring peace to tension.
Bring calm to every storm.

And Lord, touch Auntie _____'s tongue.
You know which one. In the Name of Jesus, Amen.

HOLIDAY WARFARE PRAYER #3

The Family Function Fireproofing Prayer

Lord, make me fireproof.
Fireproof from insults.
Fireproof from jealousy.
Fireproof from competitive spirits.
Fireproof from cousin drama.
Fireproof from the sibling who still sees me as I was at age 12.

Let every flaming arrow of negativity hit the floor.
Let every side-eye lose its power.
Let every slick comment dissolve in the air.
Let every spiritual attack boomerang back to hell.

Cover me with Grace.
Saturate me with Peace.
Let me glide through this function like I'm wrapped in Your Glory.
In Jesus' Name. Amen.

HOLIDAY WARFARE PRAYER #4

The New Year's Boundary-Setting Prayer

Lord, as the new year approaches,
help me set boundaries without guilt,
distance without bitterness,
clarity without conflict,
and protection without apology.

Heal me from the pressure to be everything for everyone.
Deliver me from carrying family burdens.
Prevent me from repeating cycles in a new year.

Let every unhealthy expectation fall off me.
Let every unspoken obligation be broken.
Let every attempt to shame me fall flat.

I walk into the new year with:
new Peace,
new boundaries,
new joy,
new strength,
and new emotional stability.

In the Name of Jesus, Amen.

HOLIDAY WARFARE PRAYER #5

The "Lord, Don't Let Me Backslide at This Table" Prayer

Lord…
You know my heart. You know my triggers.
You know these people.

Give me level composure, Paul-in-prison resilience,
Daniel-in-the-lions'-den level of Peace,
and Jesus-on-the-cross forgiveness.

If someone says something slick—
hold my tongue.
If someone tries me—
grab my hand.
If someone provokes me—
block my reflexes.

Keep me saved.
Keep me sane.
Keep me silent when necessary.
Keep me sovereignly protected.

And if it gets too hot—
Lord, give me the Wisdom to GET UP and go home before I lay hands in the wrong direction.

In the Name of Jesus, Amen.

HOLIDAY WARFARE PRAYER #6

The "I Refuse to Be the Family Therapist This Year" Prayer

Lord, release me from the unspoken role of: the fixer, the counselor, the mediator, the emotional sponge, the peacekeeper, or the one who "holds everything together."

I release myself from holiday therapy assignments.
They can talk to You directly.
In the Name of Jesus, Amen.

HOLIDAY WARFARE PRAYER #7

The "Remain Untouched by Shade, Pettiness & Side-Eyes" Prayer

Lord, make me immune to every side-eye,
shade-filled comment,
passive-aggressive remark,
or micro-aggression disguised as holiday cheer.

I rise above pettiness.
I rise above tension.
I rise above negativity.
I rise above every assignment sent to drain me.

I am wrapped in Grace.
I am covered in Peace.
I am unharmed by foolishness.

In Jesus' Name. Amen.

HOLIDAY WARFARE PRAYER #8

The "Love From a Distance" Prayer

Lord, help me love family from a healthy distance—emotionally, mentally, spiritually, and geographically if needed.

Let my boundaries be blessed.
Let my peace be protected.
Let my joy be secured.

I love them…
but I love myself enough to stay whole.
In Jesus' Name, Amen.

HOLIDAY WARFARE PRAYER #9

The Post-Holiday Detox Prayer

Lord, detox my spirit from anything negative or toxic
that I absorbed during the holidays—
attitudes,
comments,
tension,
family spirits,
old triggers,
childhood wounds,
and emotional residue.

Cleanse my atmosphere.
Cleanse my thoughts.
Cleanse my heart.
Cleanse my home.

I step into Peace,
I step into joy,
I step into freedom,
and I leave the rest behind.

In the Name of Jesus, Amen.

HOLIDAY WARFARE PRAYER #10

The Ultimate Holiday Survival Blessing

Lord, bless me with:
the peace of Mary,
the strength of Deborah,
the wisdom of Solomon,
the patience of Job,
and the boundaries of Nehemiah.

Cover my mind.
Cover my emotions.
Cover my spirit.
Cover my holiday season with Your Spirit.

Let Your presence fill every room I enter and every conversation I endure.
And when it's time to go—
give me the dignity to leave early and the Grace to leave well. In Jesus' Name. Amen.

THE RED SECTION
Family Interrogation Warfare Prayers

The "What Are You Driving Now?" Defense Prayer

Lord, cover me when they pretend to admire my car but are really trying to check my income bracket.

Let me answer with Grace, not insecurity, not pride, and not the urge to say, "Paid for. You want a ride or a blessing?"

Let no one ask me to drive or borrow my new car this time, especially those with no driver's license, or those who have been sipping.

Guard me from comparison,
and protect my peace from financial interrogation.
In the Name of Jesus, Amen.

The "You Still Work in the Same Place?" Deflector Prayer

Lord, shield me from the backhanded career commentary.
Give me holy amnesia to the tone in their voice.
Give me the Wisdom to say,
"Yes, I'm employed — unlike some folks I could name."

But I won't say that, Jesus.
Restrain me.
In the Name of Jesus, Amen.

The "Where Did You Get That Outfit?" Surveillance Prayer

Lord, let me not fall into their trap.
Protect me from the shade hidden behind compliments.
Give me discernment to know if they mean,
"That's cute,"
or
"That's cheap."

Let me dress in dignity, not defensiveness.
In the Name of Jesus, Amen.

The "Can I Borrow Some Money?" Protection Prayer

Lord, FIX IT.
Give me the strength to say no.
Give me the wisdom to not be an interest-free bank.
Give me holy boldness to respond with,
"I can't swing it," Lord, don't let me be a liar,
even if my wallet is looking at me like,
"You lying."

Block every emotional manipulation.
Block every guilt-trip.
Block every cousin who thinks I'm their retirement plan.
In the Name of Jesus, Amen.

The "What Did Your Kids Get for Christmas?" Armor Prayer

Lord, cover me from comparison warfare.
Whether my kids got a bike or a book,
let me not fall into financial Olympics.

Block every competitive parent spirit.
Block every attempt to measure my motherhood.
Block every holiday bragging demon.
In the Name of Jesus Amen.

The "Oh… Did Your Kid Get a New Bike?" Rebuttal Prayer

Lord, sanctify my tone
so I don't respond with,
"Yes, it is — you wanna ride it?"

Cover me from their subtle financial audits.
Let me give answers dripping in grace,
not sarcasm. In the Name of Jesus, Amen.

The "Oh… You Gained Weight?" Blocking Prayer

Lord…
Please touch their eyes, their mind, and their vocal cords
so they stop giving commentary on a body they don't
pay for, pray for, or live in.

Let their words fall flat.
Let my confidence remain unshaken.
Let my self-esteem stay in one piece.
And if I DID gain weight—
Lord, help me remember: it was by Your grace and
Chick-fil-A.

Give me the strength to respond, "I gained wisdom…
you want some?" BUT HOLD MY TONGUE, JESUS.

In the Name of Jesus, Amen.

The "Oh Wow! You Lost Weight!" Discernment Prayer

Lord, help me discern whether
"you lost weight"
means:

- *genuine compliment*
- *concern masked as shade*
- *or they're checking to see if I'm struggling, sick, or stressed*

Give me peace no matter their intention.
Let me not internalize their curiosity,
their shock,
or their hidden judgment.

Let my response be:
"Thank you — life is life-ing, but God is God-ing."
And let that END the conversation.

In the Name of Jesus, Amen.

The "Sizing Me Up From Head to Toe" Spiritual Repellent

Lord, when they scan me like TSA…
from hairline to shoe sole…
give me the serenity of someone who doesn't care.

Let their eyes bounce off me like rubber.
Let their comparison spirit dissolve.
Let their measuring tape malfunction.

Bless me with unbothered glory.
In the Name of Jesus, Amen.

The "Why Is My Body Your Business?" Armor Prayer

Lord, guard my mind from body-related comments,
both negative and "positive,"
because BOTH can be invasive.

Help me detach my worth from:
size,
shape,
numbers,
opinions,
and nosy relatives who think being observant is a
spiritual gift.

My body is not a holiday topic.
My appearance is not a conversation starter.
I am fearfully and wonderfully made—
no matter the season or the scale.

In the Name of Jesus, Amen.

The "Let Me Eat in Peace" Holiday Table Prayer

Lord, as I fix my plate:

- block every comment about carbs
- block every remark about dessert
- block every "you sure you want seconds?"
- block every nutritional inspiration demon
- block every unsolicited health prophecy

Let me enjoy this plate without commentary, judgment, or performance anxiety.

In Jesus' Name—let me EAT. Let me enjoy this meal, this holiday. In the Name of Jesus, Amen.

BONUS: Leftovers Etiquette

Lord help those who come to the dinner and bring nothing, but want to take everything home to their house. Didn't Boaz leave some leftovers for Ruth?

It's called left overs because you're supposed to leave it. Don't start none, won't be none. Don't bring none, don't take none. In the Name of Jesus.

The Ultimate "Sizing Me Up" Shutdown Blessing

Lord, as they stare…
as they observe…
as they analyze my body like a math problem…
give me Peace that passes all understanding
AND all opinions.

Let me walk into this family gathering
like a child of God,
not a contestant in a weight-loss show.

And let every sizing-up *spirit* lose its power.
I am not their project. I am not their comparison point.
I am not their body commentary buffet.
I am free. In the Name of Jesus, Amen.

BONUS: Help Me Wash These Dishes & Clean This Kitchen

LORD, don't let me be the only Martha again this holiday – the only one who knows how to wash the dishes after we have all eaten to the full.

You know we ain't gonna leave all this mess for Momma to clean up. In the Name of Jesus. Amen.

RELATIONSHIP, HAIR, HEALTH & LIFE DECISIONS

The "So... You Dating Anybody Yet?" Interrogation Neutralizer

Lord... help me.
Because when they ask "You dating anybody?"
they're not asking.
They're evaluating.
They're assessing my timeline.
They're calculating my value on the marriage stock market.

**Give me the confidence to answer without:

- defensiveness

- insecurity

- sarcasm

- or a sudden desire to flip the table**

Let me respond with Grace, Peace, and a hint of holy mystery, because it ain't none of their business. In the Name of Jesus, Amen.

The "When You Having Kids?" Fertility Fortress Prayer

Lord, shield me from intrusive womb-watchers.
Those who think my ovaries are community property,
who track my biological clock like NASA,
and ask questions that only You should answer.

Help me set boundaries with class,
not cuss words. In the Name of Jesus, Amen.

The "When Are You Having MORE Kids?" Capacity Prayer

Lord, deliver me from baby-pressure prophets.
People who want me to multiply like I'm in Genesis, but won't help babysit, won't help pay for daycare, won't help buy diapers, and don't live in my house. Grant me peace, not pressure. Wisdom, not worry.
Choices, not chatter.
In the Name of Jesus, Amen.

The "Why You Still Single?" Self-Worth Armor

Lord, cover me from singleness-shamers.
Those who act like relationship status is a moral ranking,
or like being single is a spiritual disease.

Let me remember: I am whole.
I am complete. I am chosen.
I am not on clearance. In the Name of Jesus, Amen.

"Why Did You Cut Your Hair?" Identity Protection Prayer

Lord, protect me from follicle critics.
The ones who think my hair decisions require their approval.

Block every: "It was prettier before"

- "I liked it long"
- "You look different…"
- "Why you cut it?"

Let me embrace my reflection
without absorbing their opinions.
In the Name of Jesus, Amen.

The "You Look Tired..." Emotional Ambush Defense

Lord, SOME comments are unnecessary.
This is one of them.

When they say, "You look tired,"
let me respond like a saint,
not like a sleep-deprived warrior who drove 2 hours in traffic
just to have someone insult their face.

Cover my emotions.
Conceal my under-eye circles.
And convict them, Lord. In Jesus' Name, Amen.

The "You Doing Okay Financially?" Privacy Shield Prayer

Lord, put a firewall around my finances.
Block every interrogation disguised as concern.
Protect me from nosy budgeting demons, savings-account spies, and cash-flow prophets**

Let me walk in financial privacy
and holy discretion. You are my Provider, not them.
In the Name of Jesus, Amen.

The "When You Getting a House?" Expectation Eviction Prayer

Lord, deliver me from mortgage missionaries—
folks who want me to buy property
but won't cosign,
won't help with closing costs,
won't gift me a down payment,
and won't come sweep the porch.

Let me make life decisions in Your timing,
not theirs.
In the Name of Jesus, Amen.

The "Is That ALL You're Eating?" Food-Shaming Firewall

Lord, cover my plate. Whether it's heavy or light,
full or modest, balanced or busted—

LET THEM LET ME BE.

Every comment about food—
block it. Seal it. Reject it.
Send it back to sender.
In the Name of Jesus, Amen.

The "Whatever Happened With Your Ex?" Resurrection Refusal Prayer

Lord, when they dig up my past like archaeologists:
give me the agility to dodge the conversation.

Do not let me resurrect relationships
You already buried.

Let my answer be:
"God delivered me."
Period.
In the Name of Jesus, Amen.

The "What Are You Doing With Your Life Now?" Purpose Protection Prayer

Lord, help me answer without shrinking,
oversharing,
or throwing a spiritual grenade.

Let my purpose stay protected.
Let my peace stay intact.
Let my calling stay between me and You.
In the Name of Jesus, Amen.

The "Oh, So You Think You're Better Than Us Now?" Warfare Reversal

Lord, when they confuse healing with arrogance,
growth with pride,
boundaries with betrayal,
and blessings with bragging—

Reverse their assumptions.
Protect my heart.
Defend my character.
Preserve my humility.
In the Name of Jesus, Amen.

"You Acting Funny" Reflection Prayer

Lord, help me respond gently when
"I'm acting funny" =
"I have boundaries now."

Let me embody peace
without absorbing guilt.
In the Name of Jesus, Amen.

The "When You Getting a Real Job?" Identity Anchor Prayer

Lord, anchor my identity so firmly in You
that no comment about my career shakes me.

Let me walk confidently in my calling
even when others don't understand it.
In the Name of Jesus, Amen.

The "You Changed..." Release Prayer

Lord, YES—I changed.
Thank You.

Let me receive that statement as confirmation,
not accusation.

Let change be my liberation,
not my shame.
In the Name of Jesus, Amen.

The "You Always So Sensitive" Emotional Validation Prayer

Lord, validate my emotions.
Let me not be gaslit by family members
who refuse accountability and call it sensitivity.

Help me stand in my truth,
my healing,
and my boundaries.
In the Name of Jesus, Amen.

The "What Happened to the Old You?" Deliverance Declaration

Lord, help me smile gracefully as they mourn
the version of me that tolerated nonsense.

Let the "old me" stay buried.
Let the "new me" stay blessed.
In the Name of Jesus, Amen.

The "Who Do You Think You Are?" Identity Explosion Prayer

Lord, when they ask,
"Who do you think you are?"
let me stand tall and declare inwardly:

I am chosen. I am redeemed.
I am healed. I am anointed.
I am evolving. I am Your child.

And I will NOT shrink for anyone.
In the Name of Jesus, Amen.

The "You Still in School?" Educational Endurance Prayer

Lord, cover me from the academic paparazzi.
Those who track my education like a TV series.
Give me the grace to answer without aggression,
even if I've changed majors,
changed goals,
or changed my mind.

Let me remember: I'm not late. I'm not behind.
I'm on Your timeline.
In the Name of Jesus, Amen.

The "When You Gonna Finish?" Patience Prayer

Lord, deliver me from degree detectives.
They don't pay my tuition,
study my chapters, submit my assignments,
or carry my stress.

Let my progress be my business.
Let my timeline be my own.
And let my response be seasoned with peace—
not pettiness.
In the Name of Jesus, Amen.

The "Are You Still a CPA or Whatever You Studied?" Identity Clarifier

Lord, protect me from relatives who ask career questions as if I'm on trial.

Whether I stayed in the field,
left the field, or burned the field down—

Let me stand firm in my calling.
Let their tone not shake my value.
In the Name of Jesus, Amen.

The "Is That Your Real Hair?" Self-Confidence Shield

Lord, cover me from follicle interrogators.
Those who cannot greet me
without conducting a scalp investigation.

Whether it's mine, bought, blessed, or braided—
let them mind their business.
Let my confidence stay intact.
In the Name of Jesus, Amen.

The "Is That Your Real Hair Color?" Personal Space Protection Prayer

Lord, give me strength.
Because when they ask about hair color,
they're not just asking about pigment—
they're asking about identity, finances, stress level,
and possibly my salvation.

Let me answer with calmness,
not clapback energy.
In the Name of Jesus, Amen.

The "Oh, Your Husband Didn't Come With You?" Independence Prayer

Lord, protect me from marital attendance police.
Those who think my spouse's absence
means my marriage is struggling,
my home is in flames,
or I'm hiding something.

Give me a peaceful, simple answer:
"He's fine. I'm fine. We're fine."
In the Name of Jesus, Amen.

The "Your Kids Doing Okay in School?" Gradebook Privacy Prayer

Lord, cover me from academic auditors
who want updates on my children's GPA
more than they want to pray for them.

Let me protect my kids from performance pressure.
Let me not feel judged based on report cards.
Let me answer simply and gracefully:
"They're growing. God is faithful."

In the Name of Jesus, Amen.

The "So... Why Your Child Got That Gift?" Comparison Disarming Prayer

Lord, protect me from gift-judgers
who examine my child's toys
like they're appraising assets.

Let me parent with confidence
and ignore every sideways look.
In the Name of Jesus, Amen.

PRAYERS FOR WHY YOU DON'T WANT TO GO HOME FOR THE HOLIDAYS

What holiday?

Any holiday. Every holiday and sometimes there is no holiday, but an event and you are dreading going there. Why?

Honor thy father and thy mother—that's a commandment. And the Word says we should not forsake the assembling of ourselves together.

Oh, isn't that about churches?

Yes, but why are parents so fond of all the kids being there together it it weren't also about families?

"Lord, I Don't Want to Go Because My Peace Is Too Expensive"

Lord… this year, my peace is priceless.
The cost of losing it is too high.

I'm not avoiding family.
I'm protecting my sanity.
I am guarding the healing that took years for me to build.
I am choosing peace over pressure.
Rest over chaos.
Wholeness over obligation.

Give me the courage to say no,
the confidence to rest,
and the freedom to choose what nourishes my soul.

In the Name of Jesus, Amen.

"Lord, I Don't Want to Go Because I'm Tired of Being Triggered"

Lord, You know the memories there.
You know the wounds.
You know the dynamics that pull me backward,
into a younger version of myself I fought hard to outgrow.

I don't want to be triggered.
I don't want to fight old battles.
I don't want to relive trauma disguised as a gathering.

Cover me in wisdom.
Affirm my boundaries.
And remind me that avoiding pain is not rebellion —
it's self-respect.

In the Name of Jesus, Amen.

"Lord, I Don't Want to Go Because I'm Always the One Giving, Not Receiving"

Lord, I'm tired of being the emotional support system for people who don't support me.

I'm tired of pouring
into dry wells, into people who don't pour back,
into situations where I seem to always leave empty.

Give me permission to refill. Give me permission to rest. Give me permission to choose myself without guilt.

In the Name of Jesus, Amen.

BONUS: "Lord, Deliver Me From Parents, Aunties, Uncles & Elders Who Still Blame Me For Stuff I Didn't Do and that I am Not Responsible for that happened in Childhood."

Deliver me from the side-eyes of the old folks who blame me for the stuff *their* kids did, but either the kids or the parents blamed me for it back in the day.

Lord show them the Truth so they don't have to wait until Jesus comes to learn that I didn't do **that**.

Yeah, that's the whole prayer. In the Name of Jesus. Amen.

"Lord, I Don't Want to Go Because I'm Not the Same Person I Used to Be"

Lord, I've changed.
I've grown.
I've healed.
I've matured.
I'm not who I was.

But when I go home,
they treat me like the old me—
the quiet one,
the strong one,
the one without boundaries,
the one who tolerated everything.

Help me protect the new me
from environments that only remember the old me.

In the Name of Jesus, Amen.

"Lord, I Don't Want to Go Because I Feel Alone When I'm There"

Lord, sometimes being in a house full of people
is lonelier than being by myself.

Sometimes being "home"
magnifies what's broken,
not what's beautiful.

Heal the loneliness that comes from being
misunderstood,
misjudged,
or unseen by family.

Surround me with Your presence and Your comfort this season.

In the Name of Jesus, Amen.

"Lord, I Don't Want to Go Because the Conversations Drain Me"

Lord, I am tired of the questions.
The comparisons.
The gossip.
The interrogations.
The sideways comments wrapped in fake concern.

Give me strength to decline the invitation
without feeling obligated to explain my decision.

Protect my emotional energy.
Shield my spirit.
Renew my joy.

In the Name of Jesus, Amen.

"Lord, I Don't Want to Go Because I'm Healing From Them"

Lord…
I am healing from the people waiting at that table.
From the jokes.
From the criticism.
From the silent judgments.
From the roles I was forced into.
From the dynamics that harmed me.

Give me space to keep healing
without reopening wounds I'm trying to close.

In the Name of Jesus, Amen.

"Lord, I Don't Want to Go Because They Don't Respect My Boundaries"

Lord, You know the truth:
No matter what boundary I set,
they cross it.
They question it. They push against it.
They minimize it. They guilt-trip me for needing it.

I refuse to feel bad for protecting my heart.
Help me hold my ground with grace and confidence. In the Name of Jesus, Amen.

"Lord, I Don't Want to Go Because I'm Better When I Stay Away"

Lord, I'm simply healthier when I'm not there.
Calmer. More stable. More joyful. More rooted.
More myself.

Let me honor the environments where I flourish
and release the ones that drain me.

Give me wisdom to choose what strengthens my soul. In the Name of Jesus, Amen.

"Lord, I Don't Want to Go Because I Don't Want to Pretend Anymore"

Lord, I'm tired of acting like everything's fine
when it's not.
I'm tired of smiling through discomfort.
I'm tired of shrinking myself to survive the room.
I'm tired of pretending the tension isn't real.

Give me permission to be honest with myself.
Give me permission to honor my truth.
Give me permission to decline
without emotional punishment.

In the Name of Jesus, Amen.

IT *IS* A BEAUTY PAGEANT — but for SURVIVAL, not crowns.

And the worst part?
You didn't even enter the competition.
Somebody else did.

YOU just showed up to make your mother and father happy on the holiday. Well, for that and the food.

"Lord, I'm Smiling Like It's a Beauty Pageant and I Didn't Even Sign Up"

Lord…
Give me the strength to hold this polite smile
that is starting to feel like a facial cramp.

I'm over here giving Miss Congeniality energy,
but I didn't enter this pageant.
I didn't rehearse for this event.
I didn't sign up for this competition.
These people turned this holiday into the Miss Holiday Gala,
and I'm the unwilling contestant.

Lord, give me the endurance to smile through the comments, glide past the shade, pose through the interrogation, wave gracefully at the foolishness, and answer questions like I'm representing the whole state of Sanity.

Give me the poise of a queen
and the patience of a saint
as I walk through rooms filled with relatives
who think everything is a runway
and everybody is a judge.

Help me keep my crown on straight,
even if it's imaginary,
and help me respond to every comment

with Your Grace—
not my reflexes.

And when I reach my limit,
escort me out with dignity
before they see the REAL talent portion:
me leaving.

In Jesus' Name, Amen.

CULINARY INTERROGATION & BACKHANDED COMMENTS

"Lord, They Just Asked If I Cooked This"

Lord, when they ask,
"Did YOU cook this?"
in that tone…
the one with suspicion,
judgment,
and low expectations…

Give me peace.
Give me patience.
Give me pride in my recipe,
even if it came from TikTok
or Jesus Himself whispered it to me.

Let my food be seasoned,
my words be seasoned,
and their attitude be unseasoned.

In the Name of Jesus, Amen.

"Lord, They Staring at the Food Like It's an Alien"

Lord, when someone asks,
"What IS this??"
as if I served them a plate from Mars…

Calm my spirit.
Help me not respond with,
"It's called flavor — you should try it sometime."

Let my culinary creativity not be insulted.
Let my appetite not be ruined.
Let my patience not be tested by picky palates.

In the Name of Jesus, Amen.

"Lord, Why They Asking What I Put in It Like It's a Crime Scene?"

Lord, when they ask,
"What did you put in this?"
with deep suspicion…
as if I'm the FBI's most-watched chef…

Give me strength.
Give them courage.
Give us peace at this table.

Let me say ingredients,
not insults.
Let me give clarity,
not clapback.

And Lord…
if they don't like it,
let them quietly get something else.

In the Name of Jesus, Amen.

"Lord, They Just Asked Me 'What Is Anise?'"

Lord, bless them.
Because they don't know
that anise is a spice,
not a warning.

Give me the patience to explain
without rolling my eyes,
sighing dramatically,
or saying
"It's like licorice — but grown-up."

Help me educate without irritation.
Help them taste without hesitation.
Help this recipe not cause confusion
or conflict.

In the Name of Jesus, Amen.

"Lord, They Just Called Me Weird…"

Lord…
cover me.
Because when they call me "weird,"
what they really mean is
"I don't understand you,"
"I can't categorize you,"
or
"You're different in ways I wish I could be."

Give me peace in my uniqueness.
Give me confidence in my personality.
Give me strength to not absorb their small-mindedness.

Let me wear "weird" as a compliment.
Let me flourish anyway.
And let their opinions fall flat like stale cornbread.

In the Name of Jesus, Amen.

BONUS PRAYER — "Lord, Protect Me From People Who Don't Season Food"

Lord, if they ask too many questions
because they don't recognize seasoning…

Give me strength not to judge.
Give them vision to see beyond salt and pepper.
Let them taste and see that the food is good.

And if they STILL complain…
give me the Grace to let them eat from the kids' table.

In the Name of Jesus, Amen.

KITCHEN WARFARE: THE EXTENDED EDITION

"Lord, They Just Said 'Who Made the Potato Salad?'"

Lord…
You already know that in certain cultures,
this question is not innocent.
It is a warning.
A threat.
A whole spiritual inquiry.

Give me peace as I answer.
Give me wisdom to say "I did"
without fear or trembling.

And Lord…
if they don't like my potato salad—
let them skip it silently.
In the Name of Jesus, Amen.

"Lord, They Just Said, 'Why Does Your Food Look Like That?'"

Lord, be my strength.
Because culinary disrespect is a temptation.

Help me not respond with:
"It looks like flavor.
Something you're unfamiliar with."

Bless their eyes. Bless their taste buds.
Bless their silence. In the Name of Jesus, Amen.

"Lord, They Said 'This Tastes… Interesting.'"

Lord, give me the serenity
to accept this backhanded compliment,
the courage not to clap back,
and the wisdom not to snatch the plate.

Give me discernment to know
when "interesting" =
"I don't like it but don't want to start a fight."

Let peace reign in my kitchen and in my heart.
In the Name of Jesus, Amen.

"Lord, They Asked If I 'Even Know How to Cook.'"

Lord, I feel the spirit of disrespect rising.
Restrain me.
Renew me.
Reboot me.

Help me not throw the dish.
Help me not throw the shade.
Help me not throw my whole personality at them.

Let my cooking speak for itself.
And let their plate stay empty if their mouth stays messy.
In the Name of Jesus, Amen.

"Lord, They Said 'My Mama Doesn't Make It Like This.'"

Lord, bless their mama.
Bless their palate.
Bless their confusion.
Bless their inability to appreciate new things.

Let me respond with class,
not a culinary clapback like:
"Well your mama should've taught YOU how to cook."

In the Name of Jesus, Amen.

"Lord, They Put Raisins in Their Potato Salad and Now I'm Concerned"

Lord… grant me strength. Grant me grace.
Grant me wisdom.

Because this is not just a cooking issue.
This is a spiritual matter. A generational matter. A warfare matter.

Help me keep my comments sacred,
my expressions neutral, and my distance appropriate.

In the Name of Jesus, Amen.

THE GUILT TRIP PRAYER SERIES

"You Didn't Get Momma a Gift?"

That question carries emotional manipulation, shame, blame, and family hierarchy politics.

"Lord, They Just Said, 'You Didn't Get Momma a Gift?'"

Lord, cover me.
Because this isn't really a question.
This is an accusation.
A setup.
A guilt grenade tossed into the room.

Give me the peace to respond calmly
and not explain myself to people
who don't contribute to Momma's needs
but want to monitor MY generosity.

Help me remember:
Gifts are optional.
Guilt is not of God.
Pressure is not my portion.

In the Name of Jesus, Amen.

"Lord, They Want to Compare Gifts Now..."

Lord, save me from the comparison committee.
Those who want to measure love
by price tags,
Amazon orders,
or who bought what.

Break this gift-measuring spirit.
Break this competition.
Break this pressure.

Let me give in peace
or not give at all—
without shame.

In the Name of Jesus, Amen.

"Lord, I'm Being Guilt-Tripped About Not Buying Enough"

Lord, when they say things like:
"That's ALL you got her?"
"Wow… interesting…" "That's it?"

Help me not feel inadequate.
Help me not feel judged.
Help me not feel obligated.

Bless my heart, not my receipts.

In the Name of Jesus, Amen.

"Lord, They're Making My Gift About THEM"

Lord, remove me from the emotional circus.
This is not about the gift.
This is about control. About attention.
About drama. About projection.

Help me detach. Help me breathe.
Help me smile without snapping.

In the Name of Jesus, Amen.

"Lord, I'm Just Trying to Celebrate—Not Get Shamed"

Lord, let this holiday be about love,
not guilt.
About presence,
not presents.

Help me enjoy the day
without being dragged into
family expectations
or adult peer pressure.

Let peace be my gift this year.
In the Name of Jesus, Amen.

"Lord, They Just Said: 'Why Didn't You Call Momma?'"

Lord... cover me.
Because this sentence is not a question.
It is an ambush.
A trap. A spiritual subpoena.

They didn't ask, "Is everything okay?"
They didn't ask, "How have *you* been?"
They didn't ask,
"What happened?"

No, Lord.
They attacked first, discerned later.

Give me grace.
Give me clarity.
Give me peace.
Give me the strength to NOT explain my entire
emotional history
to someone who has never called ME.

Lord, liberate me from the guilt they're trying to deliver
like a certified package.

Let me move in compassion,
not compulsion. In sincerity,
not shame. In real connection,
not fear of judgment. In the Name of Jesus, Amen.

"Lord, They Said: 'Momma Misses You.'"

(Translation: "We're guilt-tripping you again.")

Lord, help me discern
whether Momma actually said it
or they're using her name
to manipulate my emotions.

Give me the courage to reach out
when I'm ready,
not when guilt demands it.

Help me love from wisdom,
not obligation.
IAmen.

"Lord, They Said: 'Momma Was Asking About You...'"

Lord, You know the truth.
Sometimes that means Momma said,
"How's everybody doing?"
and they twisted it into
"She asked specifically about YOU."

Give me discernment.
Give me boundaries.
Give me the ability to verify the source
before absorbing the guilt. In the Name of Jesus, Amen.

"Lord, They Said: 'Momma Worried About You'"

Lord…
I'm grateful for genuine concern. But deliver me from fake worry wrapped in emotional manipulation.

If Momma is truly worried,
help me respond with compassion.
If they are using worry as a weapon,
help me respond with distance and holy Wisdom. In the Name of Jesus. Amen.

"Lord, They Asked: 'Why You Don't Come Around Anymore?'"

Lord, help me hold my tongue.
Because the REAL answer
would start a family earthquake.

Help me say:
"I've been busy,"
instead of:
"I don't like how I feel when I'm here."

Help me choose peace
over explanation.

In the Name of Jesus, Amen.

"Lord, They Said: 'Momma Thinks You Don't Care.'"

Lord…
heal the misunderstanding.
Heal the broken communication.
Heal the gaps created by distance,
hurt,
or stress.

But also—
help me reject false narratives
that were NEVER spoken by Momma
and ALWAYS spoken by messy family spokespeople.

In the Name of Jesus, Amen.

"Lord, They Said: 'Everybody Else Calls Momma But YOU.'"

Lord, break the comparison spirit.
Break the scoreboard mentality.
Break the family ranking system
that keeps emotional scorecards
like it's a championship tournament.

Help me honor Momma
in the way that fits my heart,
my capacity,
and my season of life—
not in the way other people demand.

In the Name of Jesus, Amen.

"Lord, They Said: 'Momma Getting Old… You Need to Do Better.'"

Lord, bless Momma. Bless her health. Bless her years. Bless her journey.

But remove from me the burden of guilt
placed by people who don't know
my schedule, my stress, or my silent struggles.

Let me show love from truth, not pressure.

In the Name of Jesus, Amen.

"Lord, They Hit Me With: 'You Know You Her Favorite…'"

Lord, deliver me from favoritism guilt,
middle-child guilt, oldest-child guilt,
youngest-child guilt,
and "chosen child" responsibilities
that I never asked for
and did not apply for.

Help me love Momma genuinely
without carrying the whole emotional load
of the entire family tree. In the Name of Jesus, Amen.

"Lord, They Said: 'Momma Cried Because You Didn't Call.'"

Lord, be with Momma.
But also, Lord…
tell the truth on EVERYBODY.

Expose whether she cried
because she misses me,
or because somebody stirred up drama
in her spirit.

Heal what's real.
Reveal what's fake.
And help me respond with compassion,
not guilt. In the Name of Jesus, Amen.

PRAYER SERIES: THE "WHO'S GONNA BE THERE?" CALL TO MOMMA

Because this call is not simple.
This call is *strategy*.
This call is *survival*.
This call is *risk management*.

You need to know WHO is coming so you can decide IF you are coming.

"Lord, Before I Commit, I Need to Know Who's Gonna Be There"

Lord…
I'm on this phone asking Momma in a whisper,
not because I'm being funny,
but because I'm trying to prepare my SPIRIT.

You know, Lord…
Certain people require armor.
Certain people require fasting.
Certain people require intercession.
Certain people require boundaries.
Certain people require…
distance.

Help Momma tell the truth.
Help her tell the FULL list.
Help her not leave off people
who magically appear at the last minute.

Give me clarity.
Give me foresight.
Give me emotional intelligence.
Give me a sign whether I should go… or stay home.

In the Name of Jesus, Amen.

"Lord, If Momma Hesitates Before Answering..."

Lord, when Momma says "Well… let me see…" or "Far as I know…" or "I THINK it's just us…"

Give me discernment. Because hesitation is a warning. Uncertainty is a red flag. And vagueness is spiritual danger.

Let me hear what she's NOT saying. Let me catch the names she avoids. And let me make wise decisions accordingly. In the Name of Jesus, Amen.

"Lord, If THAT Person Is Going to Be There..."

Lord, you know EXACTLY who I mean. That one relative who drains the room. Who asks too many questions. Who brings too much energy.
Who talks too loud, too long, and too wrong.

If THEY are going… give me Wisdom whether *I* should go. Let me not be guilted. Let me not be pressured. Let me not be trapped.

Give me peace in whatever choice I make.
In the Name of Jesus, Amen.

"Lord, If Momma Says: 'Everybody Coming...'"

Lord… that's not an answer.
That's a threat.
That's a warning.
That's a whole spiritual assignment.

Prepare my mind.
Prepare my emotions.
Prepare my escape route.
Prepare my boundaries.

Because "everybody" includes
people who should NOT be in the same room
together OR with me.

In the Name of Jesus, Amen.

"Lord, If Momma Forgets to Mention Someone... and They Show Up Anyway"

Lord, strengthen me.
Because these surprise appearances
are how emotional warfare begins.

Give me the calmness to endure. The discernment to
navigate. And the patience to avoid saying,
"Oh… YOU here?"

Help me maintain Peace even when the guest list
changes suddenly. In the Name of Jesus, Amen.

"Lord, If Cousin Chaos Is Coming..."

Lord, You know Cousin Chaos:
The one who starts arguments.
The one who drinks too much.
The one who brings drama as dessert.
The one who wants to 'talk.'
The one who wants to 'address some things.'

If they're coming, Lord—
give me Peace to stay home if I need to.
Or strength to go if You say go.

Let my emotions be untouched.
In the Name of Jesus, Amen.

"Lord, If Momma Drops a Surprise Name at the End…"

Lord… sometimes Momma saves one name for last.
The name that changes EVERYTHING.

If she waits until the last second to say,
"Oh yeah, and *so-and-so* might stop by…"

Give me Wisdom. Give me strategy.
Give me the power of polite decline.
And give me the ability to say,
'I won't make it this year,'
without guilt or explanation. In the Name of Jesus,
Amen.

"Lord, If Momma Says: 'It'll Be Nice to See You…'"

Lord, when she says this… I know what she means.
She is hoping. She is nudging.
She is tugging at my heart.

Help me balance honoring her
without betraying myself Help me choose from love,
not pressure. Help me protect my Peace
AND my relationship with Momma.

In the Name of Jesus, Amen.

"Prayer for the Courage to Say: 'I'll Think About It'"

Lord, let that phrase
be holy, final, and free of further questioning.

Let it end the conversation.
Let it give me space. Let it be respected.

Give me the strength to not over-explain.
Give me the dignity to make decisions
that protect my emotional health.

In the Name of Jesus, Amen.

"Bless Momma for Telling Me the Truth"

Lord, cover Momma.
Because she is stuck between
keeping the peace, telling the truth,
and avoiding drama.

Bless her heart
for trying to prepare me.
Bless her wisdom for warning me.
Bless her loyalty
for not letting me walk into an ambush blind.

In the Name of Jesus, Amen.

"Lord... Why Is My EX Coming to Thanksgiving Dinner at OUR House?"

Lord…
Hold me.
Because what in the cranberry-coated, cornbread-crusted, candied yam confusion…
is THIS?

Lord, I need answers.
I need a revelation.
I need clarity.

Because my spirit is disturbed.
My peace is disrupted.
My eyebrow is raised.
And my patience is missing in action.

Lord, WHY is my ex coming to Thanksgiving?"

Who invited them?
Who allowed them?
Who said yes without consulting ME?
Was this a family decision?
A group project?
A prank?
A spiritual test?
A divine comedy?
A setup?
A trap?

A relapse PREVENTION assignment?
Lord, WHAT IS THIS?

Give me the strength not to:

- flip the table,

- be angry *and* sin,

- leave the house,

- start a documentary titled "FAMILY TRAITORS,"

- or look them up and down with that silent judgment that only You can restrain.

Lord, I'm trying to be saved.
I'm trying to be sanctified.
I'm trying to stay delivered.
But THIS?
This is testing the fruit of the Spirit I barely grew this year.

Give me the grace to sit there
without reliving old wounds,
old emotions, old patterns, old arguments,
old disappointments, old versions of myself.

Give me the Peace to breathe
through the awkwardness,
the small talk,
the weird eye contact,
the family commentary,
the cousins whispering,

and the aunties staring like they watching an episode of reality TV.

And Lord…
if this ex arrived looking healed, glowing, upgraded, blessed, favored, moisturized, and spiritually evolved…
Lord… GUARD MY HEART.
Because temptation and nostalgia love to appear at the SAME TABLE.

And if they showed up looking…
the EXACT SAME as before? Kinda dusty…
Lord, GUARD MY MOUTH.
Because the comments will try to rise.

Cover me.
Keep me.
Protect me.
Restrain me.
And reveal the REASON for this surprise appearance.

Because if You didn't send them…
if this is not Your doing…
then I reject the assignment,
cancel the emotional setup,
and rebuke the chaos, in the Name of Jesus. **Amen.**

BONUS PRAYER — "Lord, Whoever Invited My Ex... Touch Them."

Lord, I don't want to gossip.
I don't want to accuse.
I don't want to judge.

I just want to *talk*.

Talk to the person
who thought THIS was a good idea.
Talk to the person
who didn't warn me.
Talk to the person
who volunteered MY house,
MY peace,
MY energy,
MY emotional history
as a backdrop for a lifetime movie.

Lord, show Yourself mighty.
Because this is above me now.

And if my ex invited themselves, Lord, speak to their heart and give them a life so that on the next holiday they will have a place to celebrate with people who really want them there.

In the Name of Jesus. Amen.

My eyes must be betraying me; what is this?
A reunion? A reboot? A spin-off? A crossover episode?
MY SPIRIT was not prepared for THIS casting choice.

Lord, give me the strength
to endure this unexpected guest appearance.

Give me the clarity to figure out, **who** invited them.

And, why they're in my kitchen laughing with my auntie, acting like this is THEIR family? And why everyone seems so comfortable--, except ME?

Lord, keep me balanced.
Keep me focused.
Keep me seated.
Keep me civil.

Because THIS is a lot.

In the Name of Jesus, Amen.

It gets worse. Why is there an empty chair on the OTHER side of the table? Why are there 12 available seats in this room? Why did they pick THIS one?
The seat closest to my PEACE?

Touch their mind, Lord.
Redirect their seat-selection anointing.
Guide them to the far side of the table,
the basement,
the deck,
or the kiddie table, if necessary.

Give me self-control.
Give me a neutral face.
Give me the ability to breathe normally.
In the Name of Jesus, Amen.

"Look who's here!" And too many had run to the door acting like they were surprised. This is such a set up and I don't appreciate it at all.

"We missed you!"
"You should come around more!"
"YOU still look good!"
"Oh, we thought y'all would get back together!"

I'm not really watching him, but I am. Look at him, in the kitchen laughing with my cousins. Cooking? …talking and seasoning food like they LIVE here.

They can't cook. They've never cooked.

Why are they opening MY fridge?
Lord, give me the self-control
Give me Peace.
Give me clarity.
Give me space.
In the Name of Jesus, Amen.

He's trying too hard. The last two years when we were married, he didn't want to come to my folks' house with me for the holidays, so why is he here now, trying to impress my family? And it looks like it's working.

My Ex Is Trying to Impress My Family

Lord…
They're telling jokes.
Helping serve the food.
Offering to pray.
Handing out napkins.
Complimenting my mother's dress.
Putting chairs away.
Acting like a model citizen.

Touch their spirit, Lord.
Because this performance is TOO STRONG.

Give me the strength to not be impressed.
Give me the strength to not react.
Give me the strength to remember
why we broke up in the FIRST place.

In the Name of Jesus, Amen.

BONUS PRAYER — "Lord... Why Did They Introduce My Ex AND My New Partner Like It's a Group Project?"

Lord...
Touch the relative who did the introduction.
Because that was unnecessary.
That was chaotic.
That was messy.
And that was a spiritual violation.

Give me strength to maintain my composure
while silently rebuking every form of awkwardness.

If I wanted this much drama I could have stayed home with my TV and Netflix.

In the Name of Jesus, Amen.

My Auntie Is Too Much: Look At Her

LORD.
INTERVENE.
Because Auntie is messy.
Not accidentally messy.
Professionally messy.
Certified messy with continuing education credits.

They said back in the day she was a clean-up woman.

She doesn't need details.
She doesn't need updates.
She doesn't need stories.
She doesn't need flashbacks.
She doesn't need ANY of this information.

Lord, shut EVERY mouth
that wants to dig up old chapters
I already burned, buried, and blessed.

And Lord…
give me the strength not to pull Auntie aside
and ask her if she wants to be the one
dating my ex next.

In the Name of Jesus, Amen.

"Lord... Why Does My Family Act Like My Ex Is Still Part of the Bloodline?"

Lord, what is this spiritual adoption?
Why are they treating my ex better
than half the relatives who actually share DNA?

Why are they hugging them?
Why are they checking on them?
Why are they offering them plates to take home?
Why are they patching them into conversations that I am not even part of?

Lord, deliver my family from attachment issues
to people who are no longer mine.

Help them LET GO.
Help them MOVE ON.
Help them accept my growth
without recruiting my past.

In the Name of Jesus, Amen.

My Ex Is Remembering Good Times That NEVER Happened

Lord…
give me strength.
Give me patience.
Give me the ability to keep a neutral face…
because WHAT are they talking about?

Lord, they are sitting at this table
describing vacations we NEVER took,
moments we NEVER shared,
romantic gestures they NEVER did,
and storylines I have NO memory of.

Lord, are THEY okay?
Or is this… spiritual fan fiction?

Give me the Peace to listen without laughing,
the Grace to nod without agreeing,
and the strength not to say,
"That's a nice fairy tale, but it wasn't with ME."

Lord, protect me from:

- false nostalgia
- revisionist history
- selective memory disorder
- fake fondness
- emotional mirages

- breakup amnesia
- and all holiday hallucinations

Because these "good times" they are remembering were NOT good.
Were NOT times.
Were NOT memories.
And were DEFINITELY not mutual.

Lord, remind my ex:
We broke up for a REASON.
And it wasn't because of all these imaginary Hallmark moments
they are suddenly narrating like a holiday special.

Give me the strength not to scream,
"What relationship were YOU in?
Because it wasn't ours!"

Lord, silence every embellished testimony.
Cancel every delusional memory.
And block every attempt
to rekindle something
that never burned in the first place.

In the Name of Jesus, Amen.

"My Ex Just Told a Story That DEFINITELY Didn't Happen"

Lord...
they are telling it with confidence.
With DETAIL.
With EMOTION.
With dramatic pauses and monologue energy.

But You and I BOTH know:
THEY. MADE. THIS. UP.

Give me strength not to challenge the story.
Give me peace not to correct the lies.
Give me wisdom not to stand up and say,
"That ain't me. That must've been your OTHER situation."

Cover my face, Lord.
Because my expressions are loud.
My eyebrows are communicating.
My side-eye is breaking free.

Calm my spirit.
Soften my glare.
Subdue my sarcasm.
And keep my mouth from exposing ALL the truth
in front of these mashed potatoes.

In the Name of Jesus, Amen.

"Lord... Why Does My Ex Think We Were Healthier Than We Were?"

Lord…
they're remembering smiles but forgetting arguments.
Remembering dates but forgetting disasters.
Remembering hugs but forgetting heartbreak.
Remembering chemistry but forgetting chaos.
Remembering the highlights but forgetting the hospital-grade lowlights.

Give me the wisdom to see illusions for what they are:
PRETEND.
A FILTER.
A PREVIEW CLIP.
Not the FULL movie.
Not the REAL relationship.

Help me stay rooted in the truth:
I didn't survive that relationship
just to romanticize it now.

In the Name of Jesus, Amen.

BONUS PRAYER — "Lord... Help Me Not Correct the Lies in Front of the Family."

Lord, restrain me.
Because the way my ex is talking…
I could EASILY expose some things.
EASILY.

But help me stay dignified.
Help me stay grown.
Help me stay healed.

And if the lies get TOO big…
give me permission to excuse myself
to the bathroom,
outside,
or my car
so I can scream in peace.

In the Name of Jesus, Amen.

The Doorbell Just Rang. My Ex's Parents Are Here. But, Why?

LORD.
LORD.
LORD.
Are You SEEING this?
Are You witnessing this??

Because my spirit is confused.
My mind is racing.
My patience is trembling.
And my boundaries are filing a complaint.

Lord…
WHY are my ex's parents at my door?

Did I order nostalgia?
Did I RSVP to trauma?
Did I subscribe to Past Relationships Monthly?

NO I DID NOT.

And yet…
here they stand.
With a red velvet cake.
With a smile.
With UNINVITED ENERGY.

Lord, I thought we were done with that whole family.
The ENTIRE family.
The whole bloodline.

The entire tribe.
All branches of the emotional ancestry.

So WHY are they here?
Who invited them?
Who approved this?
Who decided this was acceptable?
WHO gave them the address??
(Lord, You know exactly who. Touch them.)

Give me strength, Lord.
Strength not to slam the door.
Strength not to say,
"Oh absolutely not."
Strength not to whisper,
"Is this the Twilight Zone?"
Strength not to faint in front of the macaroni.

Give me CLASS, Jesus.
Give me composure.
Give me a smile that looks holy
but not too holy,
because I do not want them thinking
I am excited about this appearance.

Lord, help me navigate:

- awkward hugs

- air kisses

- long stares

- "We miss you" energy

- people treating me like the prodigal child who married into the family
- and my NEW partner watching this whole reunion unfold like a plot twist

Protect my Peace.
Protect my heart.
Protect my SPACE.
Protect my THRESHOLD.
Protect my SANITY.

And Lord…
if this is a sign
of ANY attempt
to resurrect ANYTHING
from the past —

I rebuke it in the Name of Jesus.
Politely.
But firmly.

Amen.

"Lord... Why Did My Family Let My Ex's Parents IN?!"

Lord...
please explain WHY
my family is acting like these people
are STILL my in-laws.

They're in the kitchen. They're fixing plates.
They're hugging folks. They're telling stories.
They're talking to my new partner like they're
interviewing them for a job.

LORD. THIS IS TOO MUCH.

Give me the strength
to NOT scream,
"WE. ARE. NOT. TOGETHER. ANYMORE."
in the middle of the living room.

Give me Grace
because this is embarrassing.
This is confusing.
This is spiritually chaotic.

Help me breathe.
Help me smile.
Help me not leave this whole event early.

Help me not move out of state tomorrow.

Amen.

"What If They Came to Win Me Back?"

Lord…
if this is a coordinated mission
to restore something that
YOU already ended…
shut it down IMMEDIATELY.

If they came with nostalgia, sentiment, apologies
manipulation, family pressure, or emotional flashbacks

Lord, give me discernment
to RUN THE OTHER WAY.

Let false reconciliation *spirits*
and holiday weakness
NOT enter my atmosphere.

Block every attempt
to soften my heart
through memory,
family,
tradition,
or seasonal loneliness.

Let me stay healed.
Let me stay free.
Let me stay delivered.
Let me stay GONE.

Amen.

My Ex's Parents Brought GIFTS

Lord...
THEY BROUGHT GIFTS??
Gifts wrapped.
Labeled.
Selected WITH THOUGHT??

This is not accidental.
This is not neutral.
This is not "We were just in the neighborhood."

This is an *operation*.
A coordinated effort.
A spiritual ambush disguised in tissue paper and bows.

Give me the strength
to receive gifts without receiving DELUSION.
Give me Wisdom
to not interpret generosity as destiny.
Give me discernment
to say, *thank you*
without saying "falling into any trap.

Amen.

Why Did They Say I'm STILL Part of the Family?"

Lord…
the way they smiling…
the way they talking…
the way they hugging…
the way they repeating,
"You'll always be part of this family,"
makes me want to run out the back door.

Give me the strength
to not respond with,
"Well y'all weren't there when YOUR child was acting a fool."

Give me Grace
to accept kindness
without reattaching soul ties
I worked HARD to break.

Help me be honored
without being HOOKED.

In the Name of Jesus, Amen.

They Are Taking PICTURES Like This Is a Reunion

Lord…
My ex's mama has her phone out.
My ex's daddy is posing.
My auntie is framing the shot.
My uncle keeps saying,
"Everybody squeeze in!"

LORD, WHY???

Give me the Wisdom
to smile FOR the photo
without making it look like
I want to be in the photo.

Give me the power
to break every unspoken expectation
that these family pictures
mean reconciliation.

Give me a strategy
to step OUT of these photos gracefully
before they upload them and tag me with:
"Family forever 🖤"

In the Name of Jesus, Amen.

"Lord... Why Is Somebody Crying?"

Lord…
who cried?
why?
who triggered this?
what story got told?
what memory got unleashed?

Is this actual emotion
or holiday manipulation?
Are these tears holy
or strategic?

Give me clarity.
Give me Peace.
Give me distance
if distance is needed.

And Lord—
if anyone tries to hug me
while crying about my past…
strengthen my spine.
Keep me upright.
Don't let me fold.

In the Name of Jesus, Amen.

This Feels Like an Intervention

Lord…
people are circling.
People are talking low.
People are glancing at me.
People are gathering like they practicing choreography.

This does NOT feel like a holiday dinner.
This feels like an ambush.
A meeting.
An intervention.
A family council
with MY name on the agenda.

Give me sharp discernment
to see what's being planned.
Give me quick reflexes
to escape respectfully.
Give me boldness
to shut down ANY attempt
to reopen a chapter CLOSED BY YOU.

In the Name of Jesus, Amen.

"Lord... WHY DO THEY STILL HAVE MY PICTURE UP IN THE LIVING ROOM???"

LORD.
I HAVE A QUESTION.

I just saw a picture taken today in their living room.
I looked just behind them and to the left…
looked to the right…
and THERE IT WAS.

Front and center.
Framed.
Spotlighted.
Dust-free.
Honored.
Cherished.
Displayed like a shrine offering.

Lord… WHY?

Why is MY face still up in my in-laws' house?
Why is my picture still part of the décor?
Why is it next to the diplomas and baby photos?
Why is it in the SAME FRAME as people who are STILL in the family??

Lord, this is emotional witchcraft.
Emotional sabotage.
Emotional confusion.

Give me the strength not to:

- gasp
- choke
- scream
- ask, "WHY am I still there?"
- or drive over and take the picture DOWN myself

My ex's parents need boundaries.
My ex needs closure. (Maybe he is soul tied to me.)
Lord, give me PEACE.

And Lord—
if the picture is their way of saying
"we wanted you to stay"…
heal them, Lord – restore their souls.

Because THIS is wild.

FINAL PRAYER — "Lord... Thank You for Telling Me NOT to Go That Other Time

Lord…
thank You.
Thank You for the whisper.
Thank You for the nudge.
Thank You for the feeling in my chest that said,
'Stay home this time.'

Because if I had gone?
If I had walked in that house? Or, more like an emotional ambush.
If I had stepped into that spiritual reality show
with my ex,
their parents,
their memories,
their delusions,
their casseroles,
their emotional surprise attacks,
AND my new partner watching it all…?

LORD.
I WOULD NOT HAVE MADE IT through all that drama.

Thank You for blocking the disaster
I didn't even know was waiting for me.
Thank You for protecting my Peace
before the chaos began.
Thank You for delivering me

from a holiday episode
that I did not need to be cast in.

Lord, thank You for teaching me that I don't have to attend every gathering I'm invited to. I don't have to walk into situations that disturb my Peace. I don't have to sit at tables that betray my healing. I don't have to tolerate confusion in the name of tradition. I don't have to entertain my past for the sake of politeness. I don't have to set myself on fire to keep the holiday warm.

Lord, thank You for showing me
that choosing myself is not selfish.
That protecting my heart is holy.
That honoring my boundaries is godly.
That staying home can be SANCTIFIED.

And Lord…thank You for reminding me
that Peace is a place. And sometimes that place
is my OWN couch. With my OWN food.
With my OWN quiet .
With my OWN joy.
With my OWN healing.
& With You.

In the Name of Jesus, Amen.

CLOSING DECLARATIONS

I do not fear family gatherings.
I do not dread the holidays.
I do not resent my past. I move forward and not backward. I go in the direction that God leads, not merely with human plans.
I do not carry shame for saying, "No."

I am covered.
I am healed.
I am protected.
I am discerning.
I am whole.

And I choose Peace
every time.
In every season.
In every holiday.
Without apology.

In the Name of Jesus, Amen.

DEAR READER

Not every family gathering deserves you.
Not every holiday needs your attendance.
Not every invitation is an assignment.
Not every call to "come home" is from God.

Sometimes the greatest gift you can give yourself
is the Peace you keep. That may sometimes mean
not accepting every invitation.

If you've ever felt guilty
for skipping a holiday,
avoiding chaos,
or choosing your own mental health…
let this book release you.

Choosing Peace is holy.
Choosing quiet is healing.
Choosing yourself is Wisdom.
Choosing God's leading is protection.

And sometimes,
the most anointed thing you can do
is stay home, if that is what the Lord says.

HOWEVER:

When you can process through the serious parts of this
book, and when you can laugh at the chaos,
then you can **handle the chaos.** The <u>fear</u> of holiday
chaos is often worse than the chaos itself.

But when you name it, laugh about it, pray through it, and shine a light on it— it loses its power.

And then? You can go home with Peace and boundaries, with humor, with emotional preparation and with spiritual protection. And go home with enough Grace to make Momma and Daddy happy because you made it for the holidays. :

`**You didn't remove the drama — you removed the <u>fear</u> of the drama.**

For those who get the blues over broken or lost relationships, especially during the holidays, this next prayer is for you.

I thank You, Lord,
that my EX was not the end of me—
but the END OF A SEASON.

And the EXIT was the beginning
of my freedom,
my clarity,
my destiny,
my upgrade,
my expansion,
my glow,
my peace,
my joy,
my wholeness.

Lord, I don't want anything
that doesn't want me.
I don't desire anything
You delivered me from.
I don't entertain anything
You evacuated from my life.

Thank You for the EXIT.
Thank You for the escape.
Thank You for the evolution and the elevation.

I'm better now, and I'll be better in my next relationship.

In the Name of Jesus, **Amen.**

Prayer Books by this Author

Prayer Manuals

FAKE FRIENDS: *Prayers Against Betrayers*

HOLIDAY WARFARE Prayer Manual (humorous) Surviving Family Gatherings All Year Long (without catching a case)

SOUL TIE Prayer Manual (The) Part of a 3-part series including a workbook.

MAD at DADDY Prayer Manual – part of a 3-part series including a workbook.

Healing the Sibling & Relative Wound Prayer Manual

Healing the Father-Son Wound Prayer Manual

Prayers Against Barrenness: *For Success in Business and Life*

Breaking Curses of the Mother Prayer Manual

Prayers Against Barrenness: *For Success in Business and Life*

Fruit of the Womb: *Prayers Against Barrenness*

Beauty Curses, Warfare Prayers Against
https://a.co/d/5Xlc20M

Courts of Marriage: Prayers for Marriage in the Courts of Heaven *(prayerbook)* https://a.co/d/cNAdgAq

Courtroom Warfare @ Midnight *(prayerbook)* https://a.co/d/5fc7Qdp

Prayers Against Barrenness: *For Success in Business and Life*

Fruit of the Womb: *Prayers Against Barrenness*

Beauty Curses, *Warfare Prayers Against*
https://a.co/d/5Xlc20M

Courts of Marriage: Prayers for Marriage in the Courts of Heaven *(prayerbook)* https://a.co/d/cNAdgAq

Courtroom Warfare @ Midnight *(prayerbook)*
https://a.co/d/5fc7Qdp

About the Author

Dr. Marlene Miles writes from a place of lived experience, personal healing, and a deep desire to see others whole. She knows what it feels like to carry painful words, to struggle with identity, and to long for God to rewrite the story. Through her journey, she discovered the power of prayer, reflection, and Scripture in transforming the heart.

Today, she shares those revelations with others—helping them break cycles, heal emotionally, and discover the beauty of God's truth over their lives. Her ministry flows with gentleness, honesty, and a prophetic sensitivity that reaches hearts right where they are.

Her calling is to help the broken become whole, the weary find rest, and the wounded step into purpose. Every book she writes is an offering of healing, hope, and freedom.

www.ingramcontent.com/pod-product-compliance
Lightning Source LLC
LaVergne TN
LVHW051558080426
835510LV00020B/3038